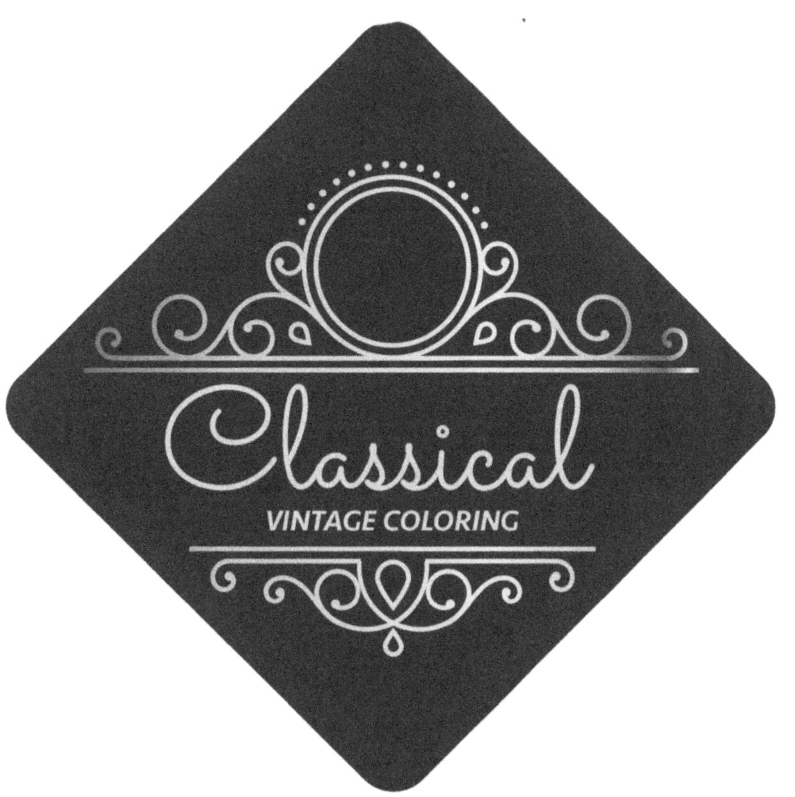

Coloring books for adults. Vintage fairies, vintage flowers, vintage animals and more!

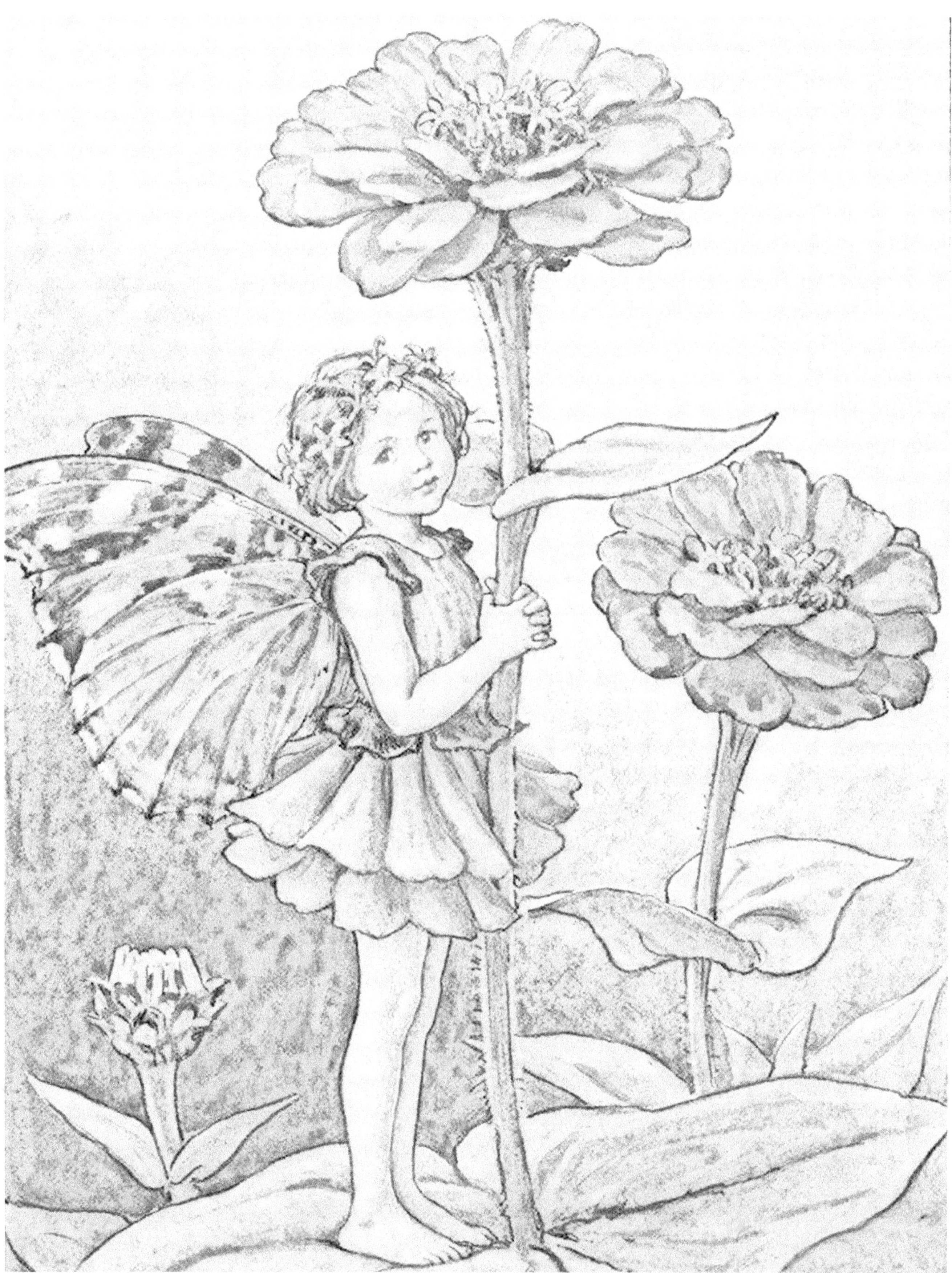

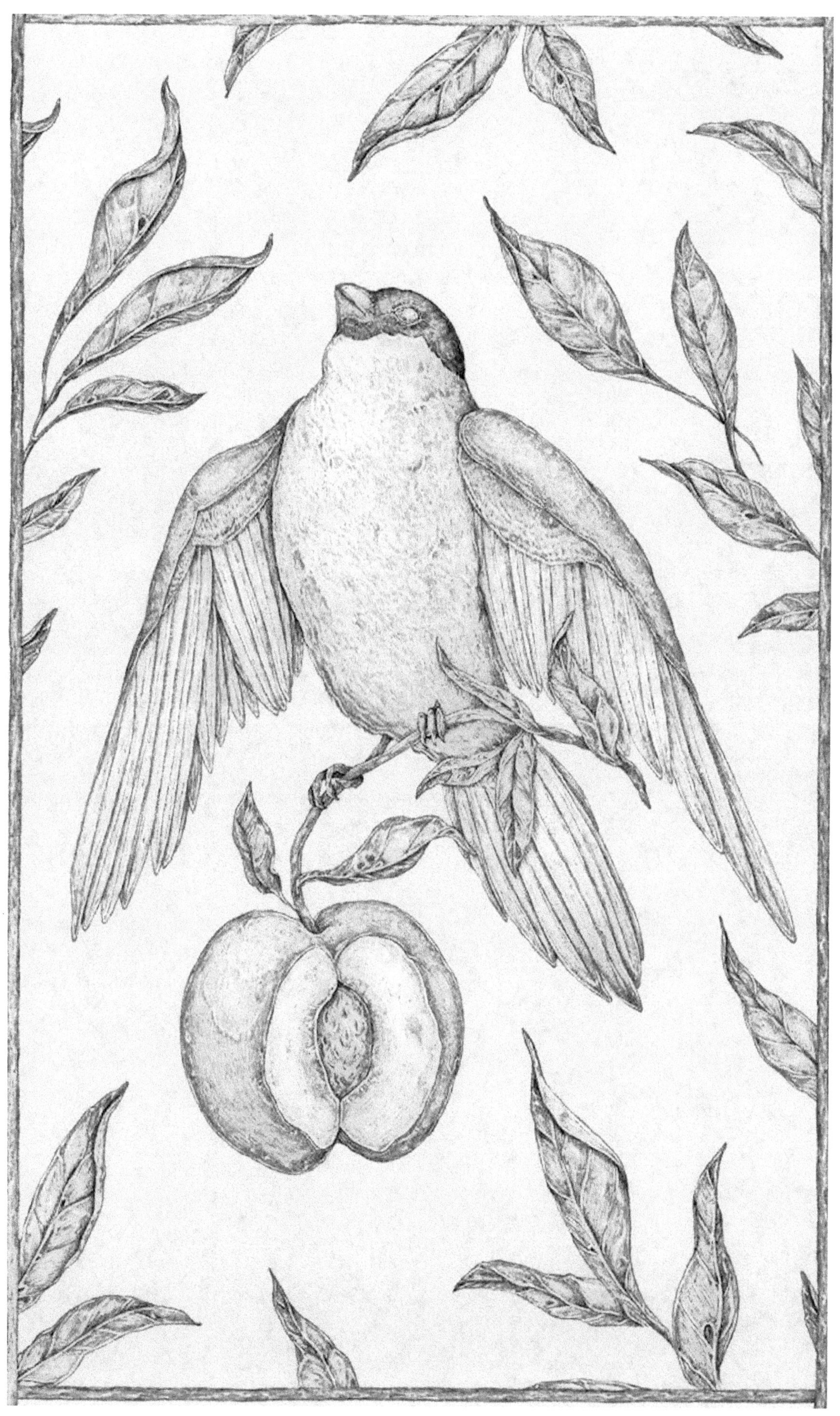

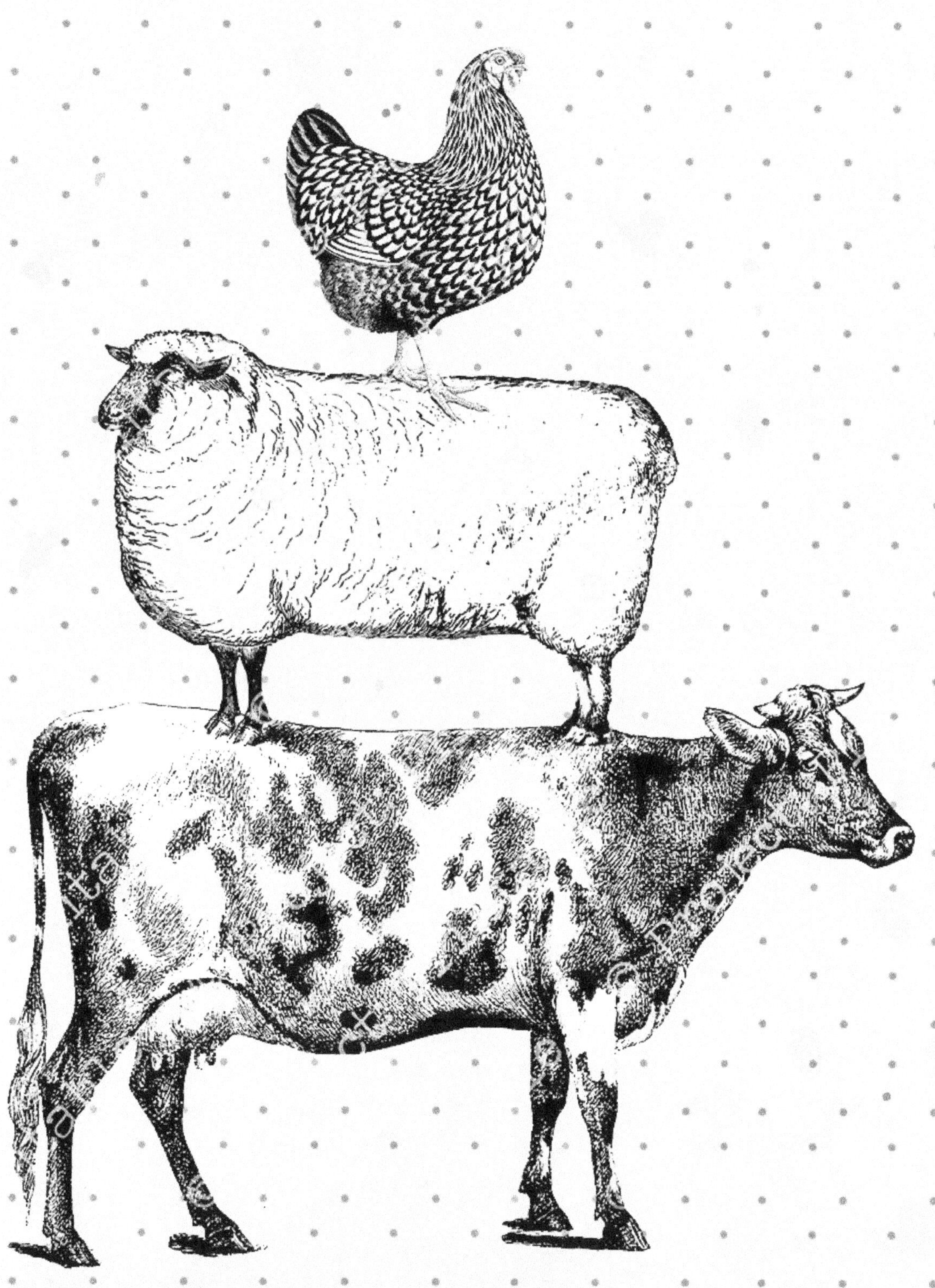

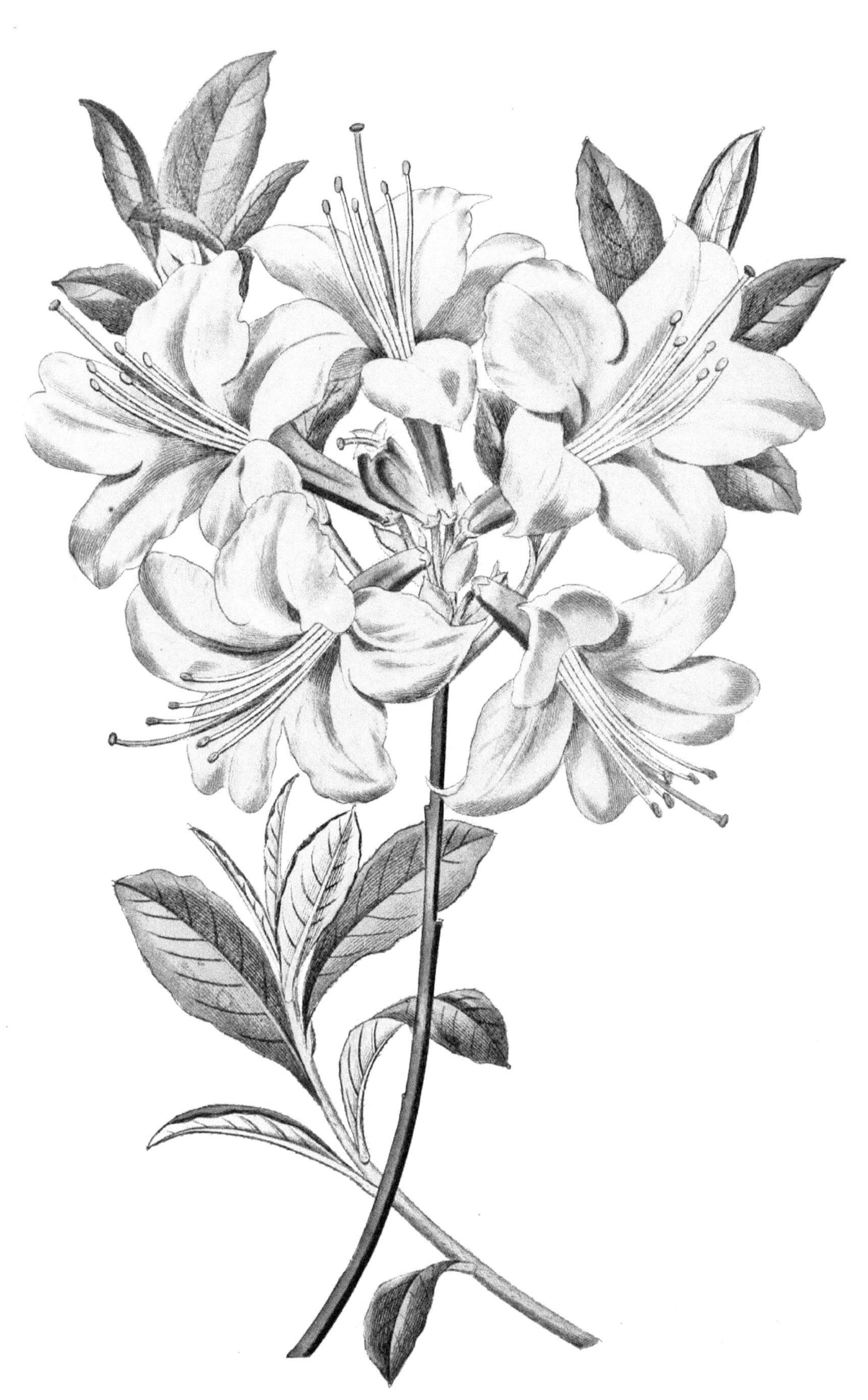

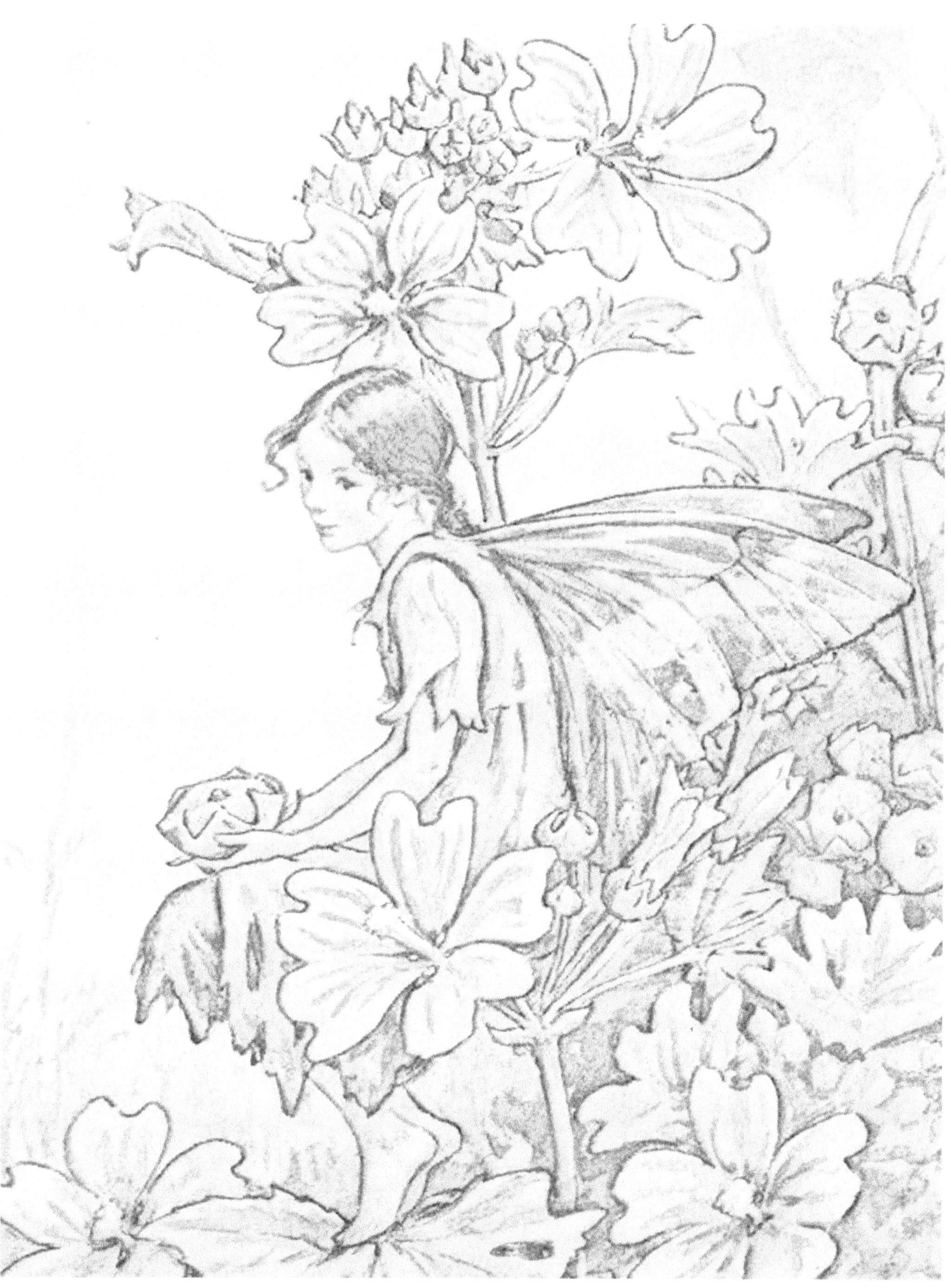

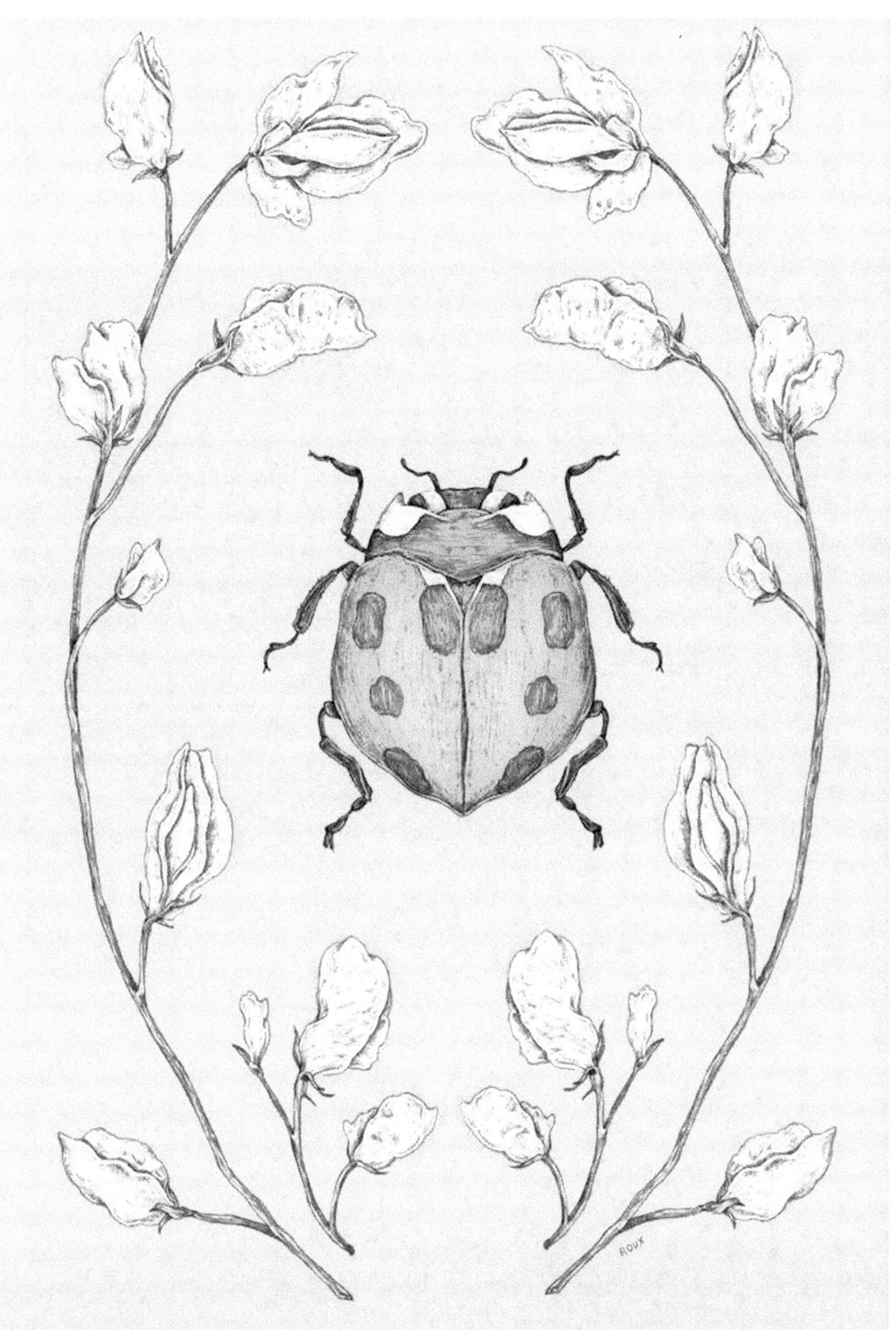

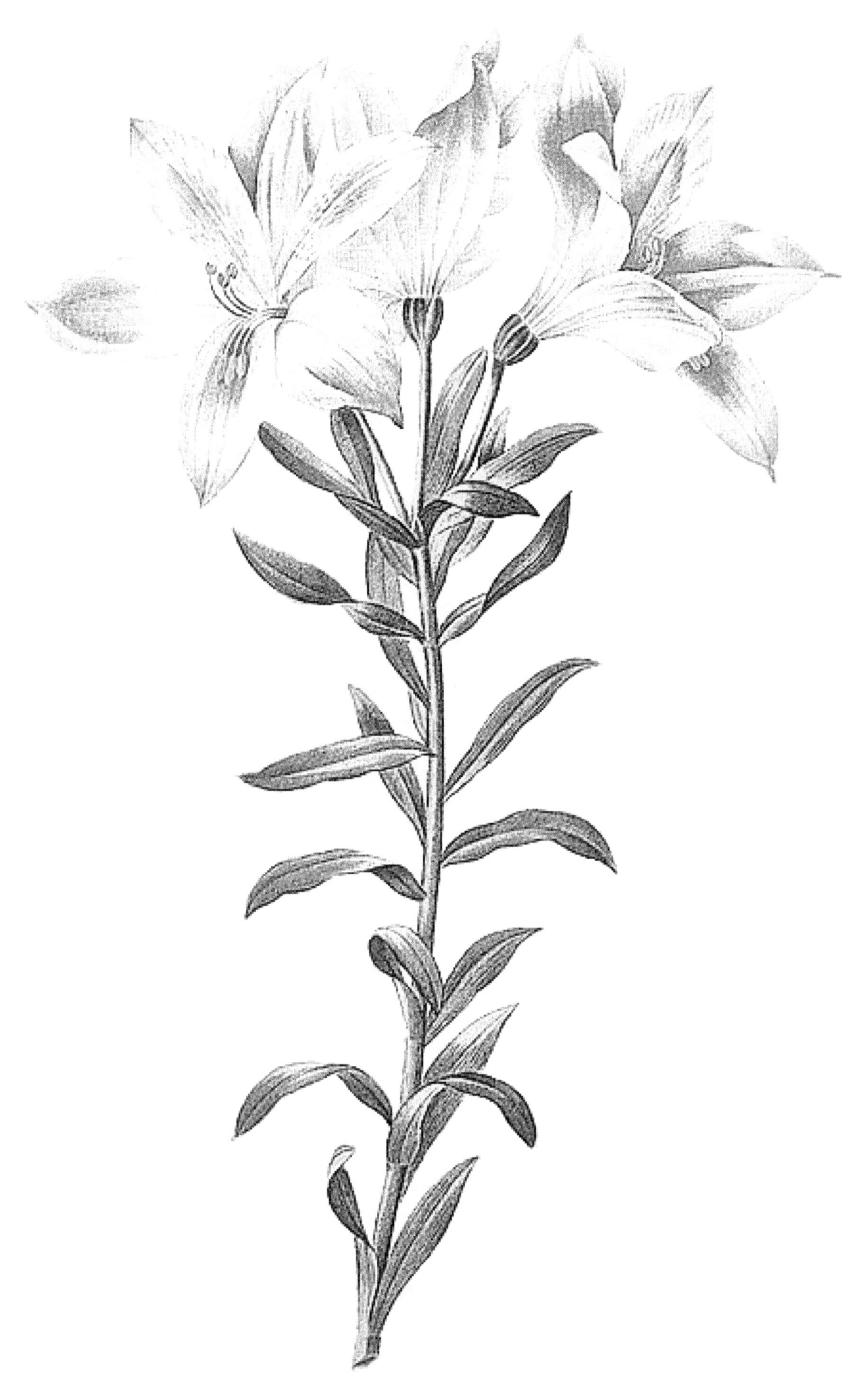

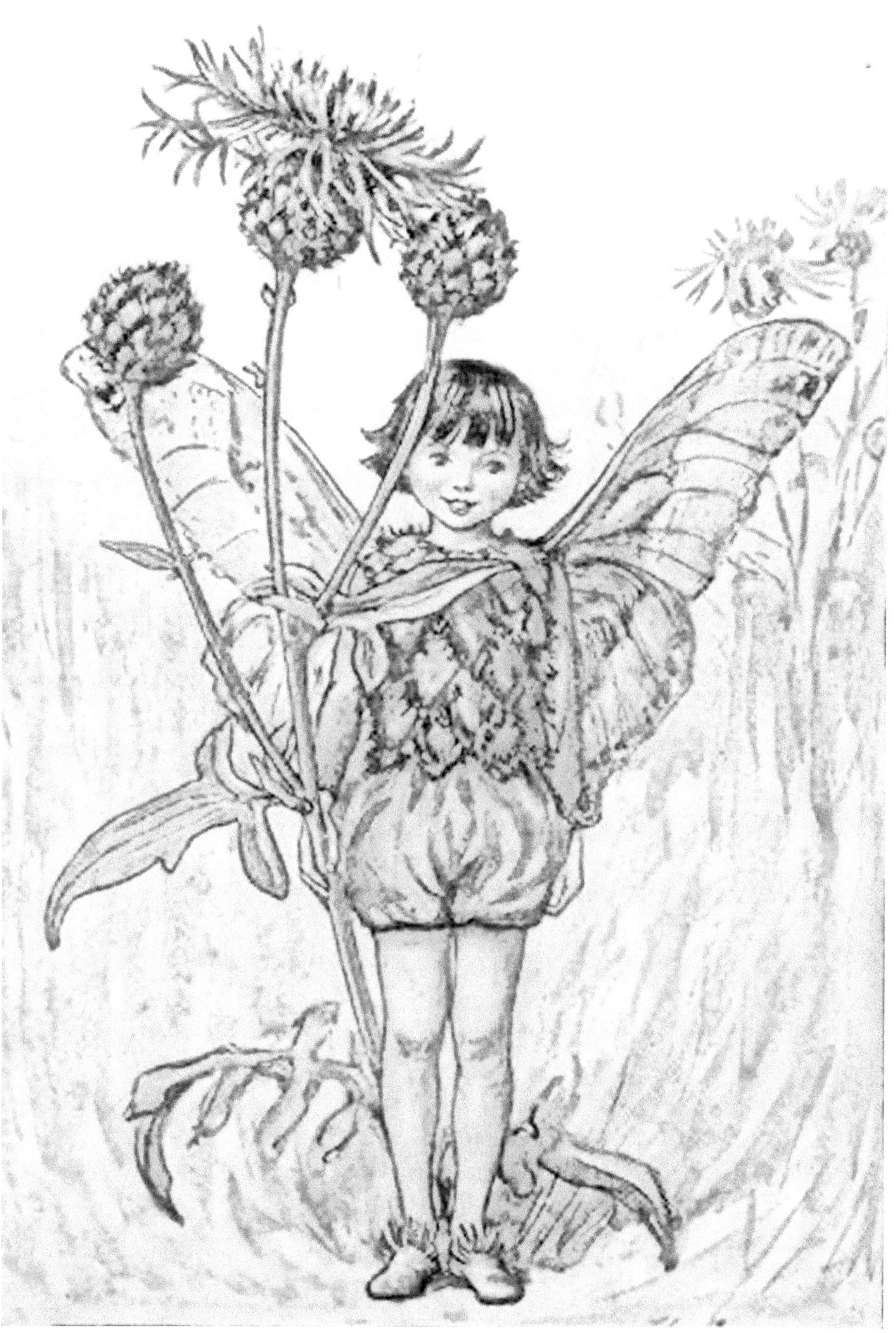

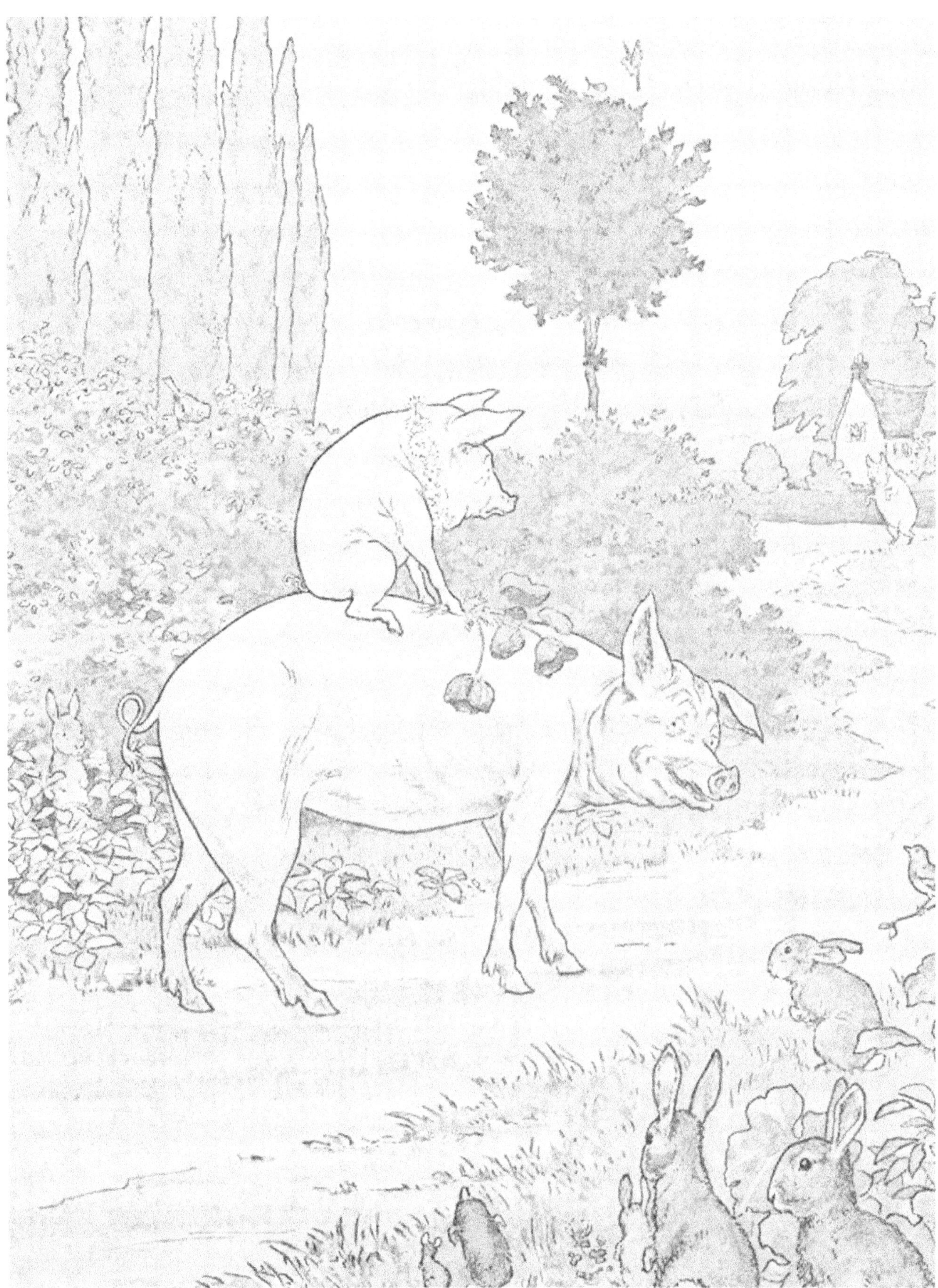

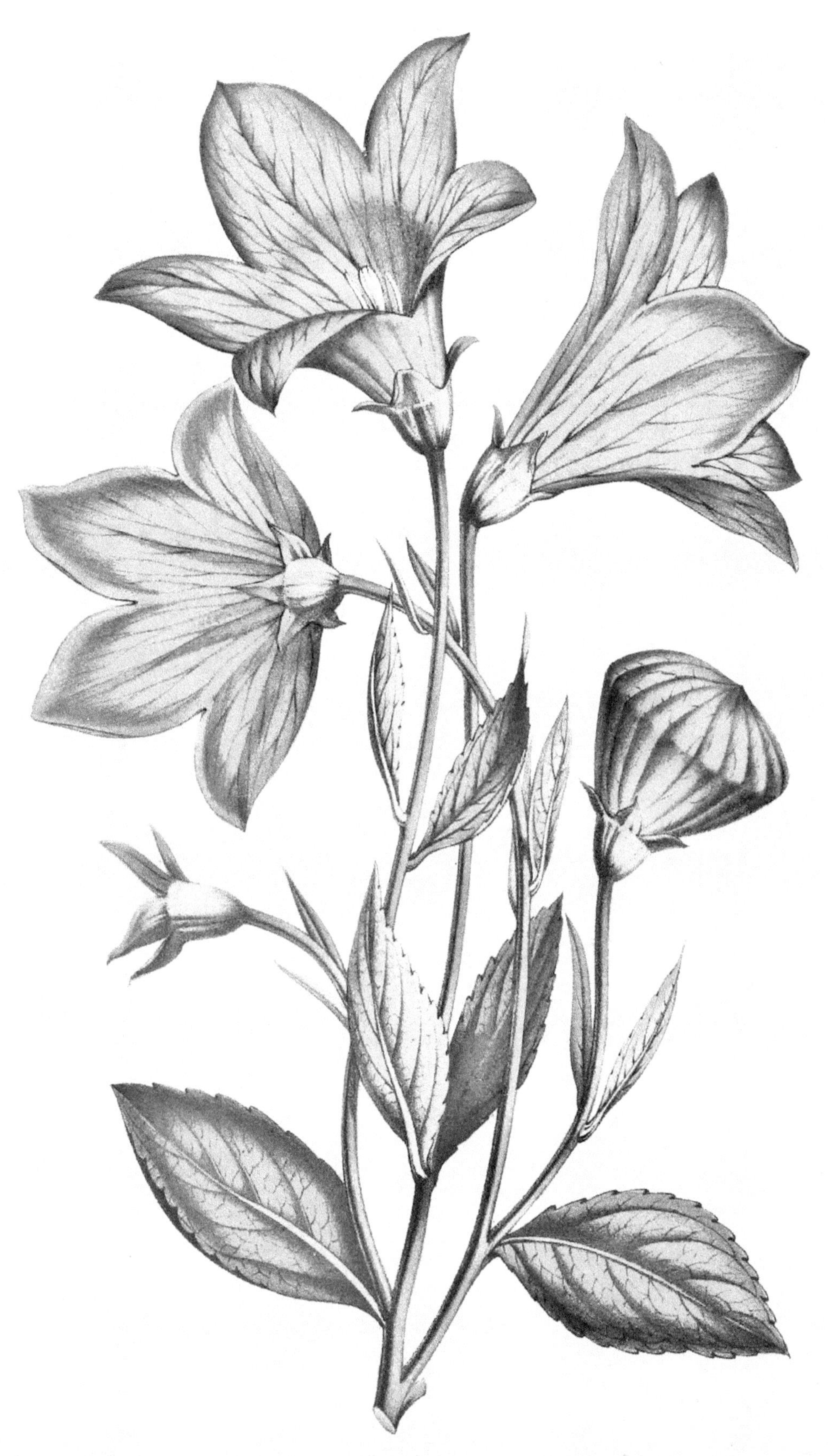

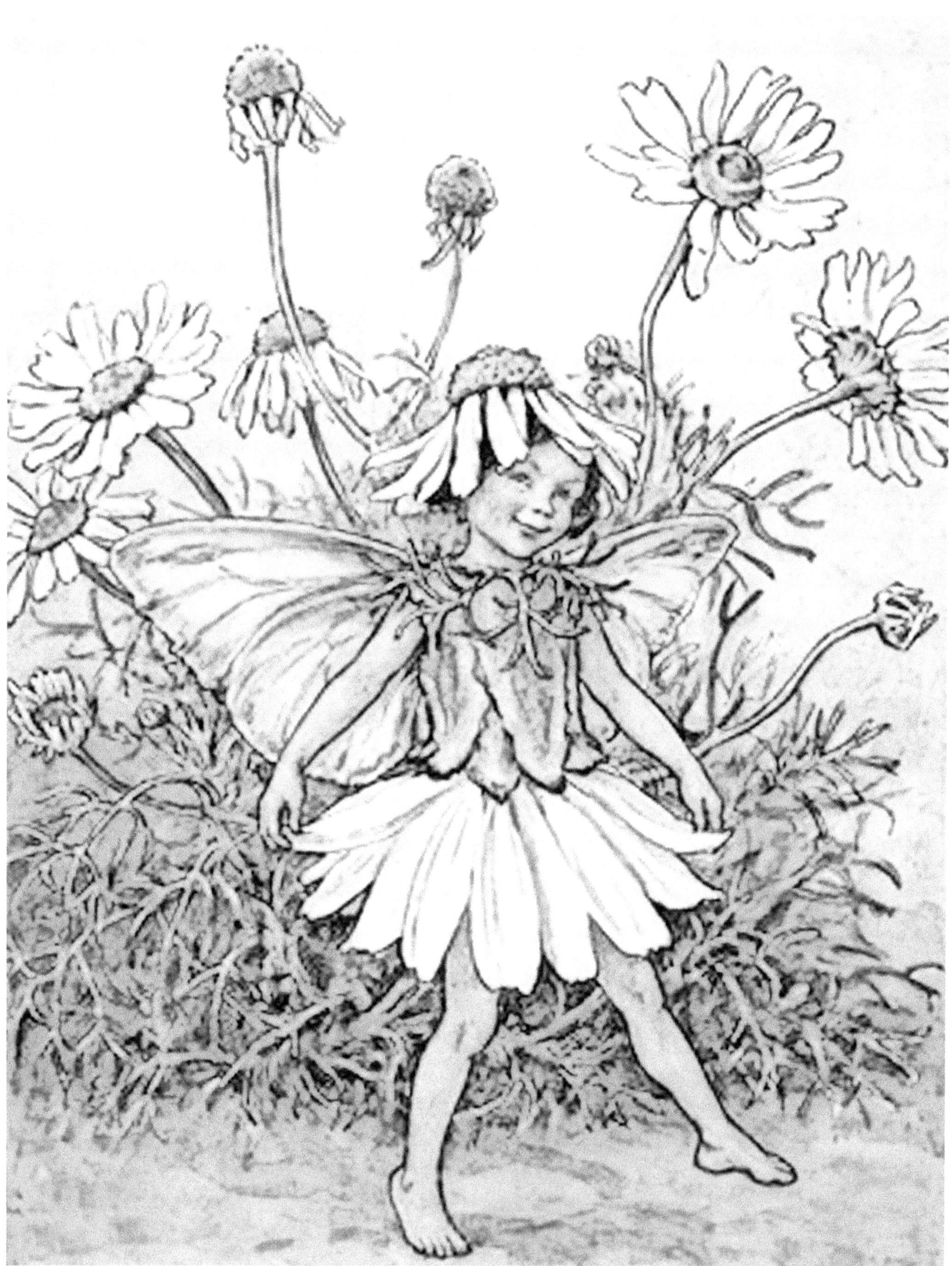

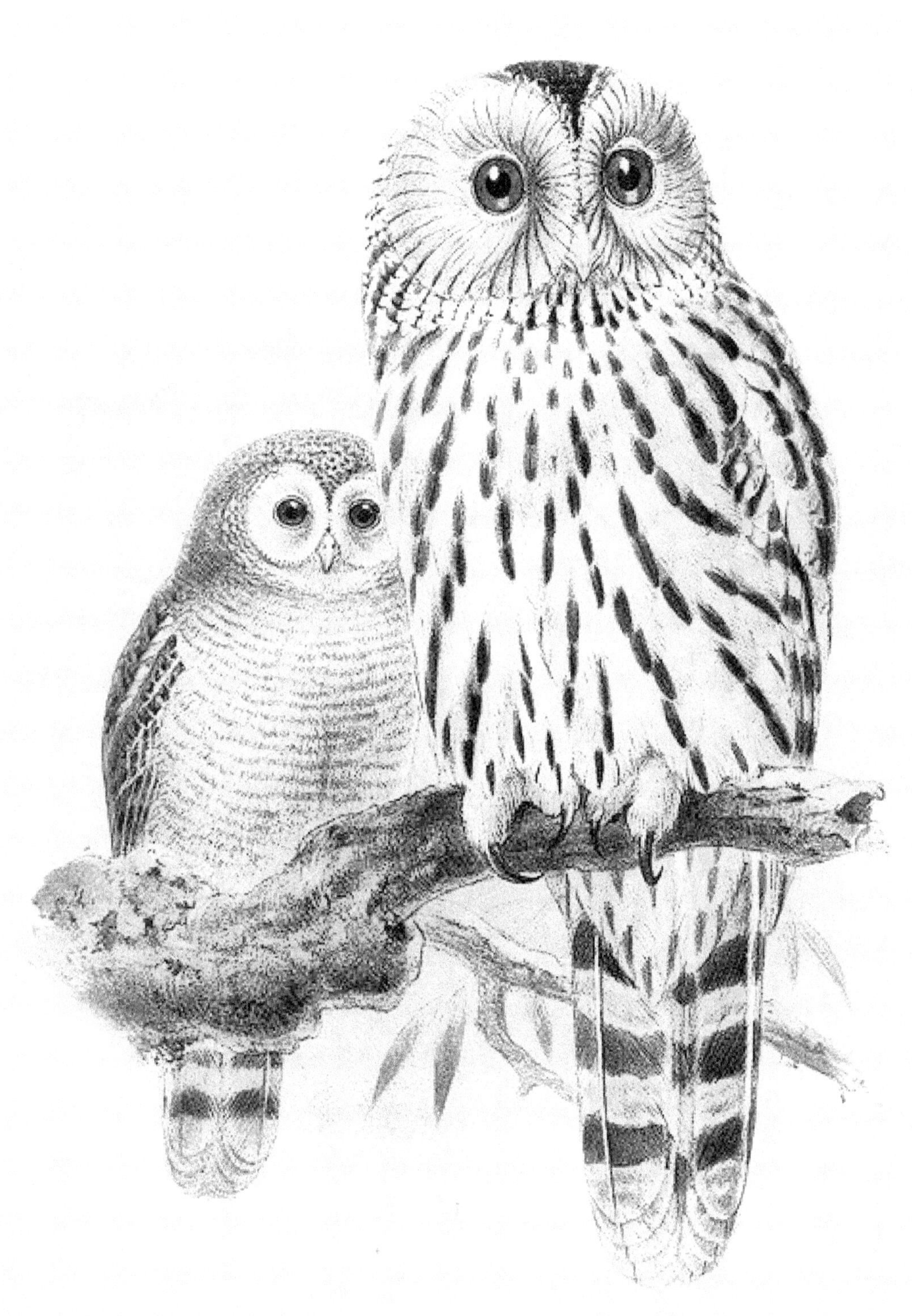

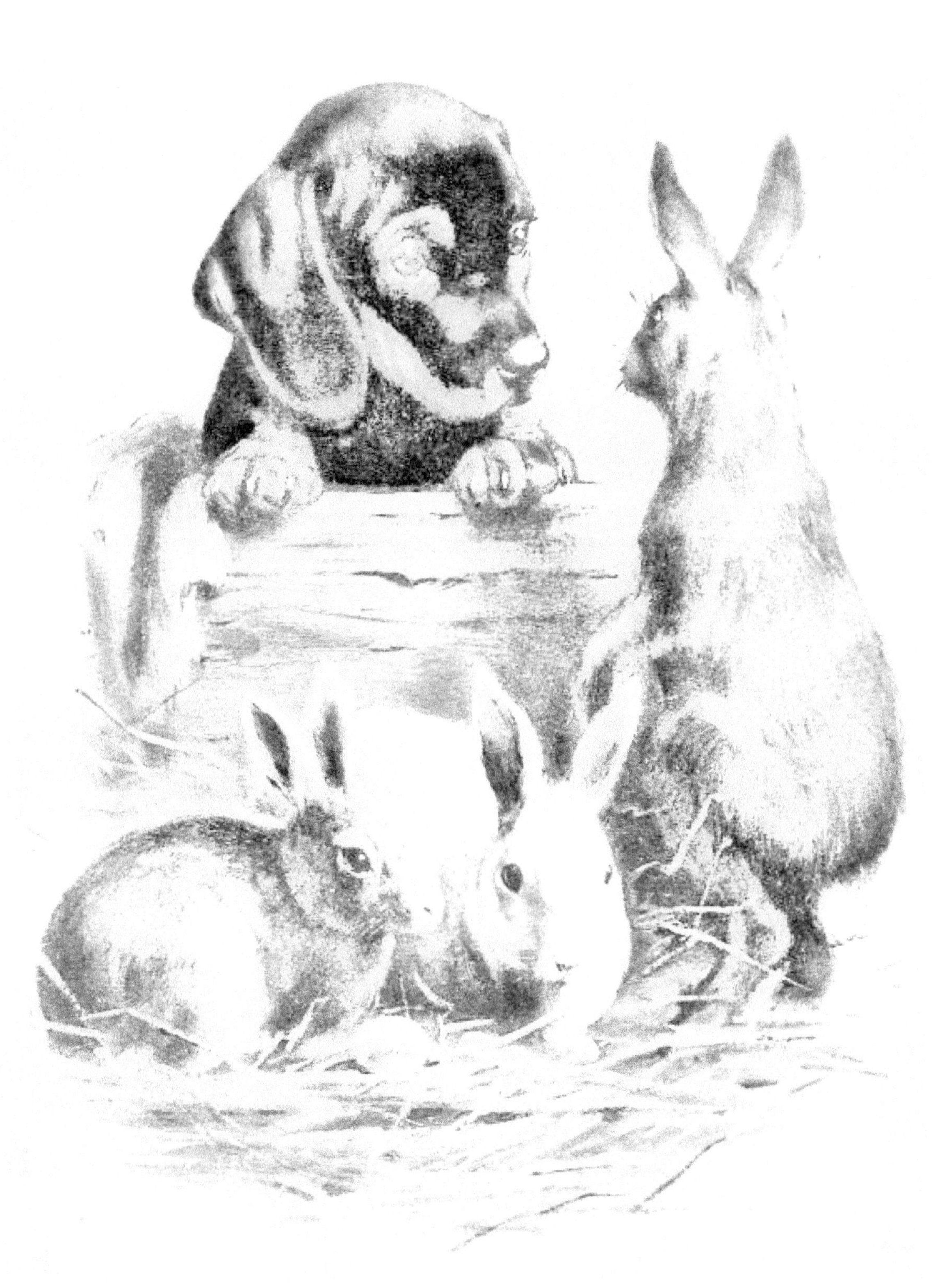

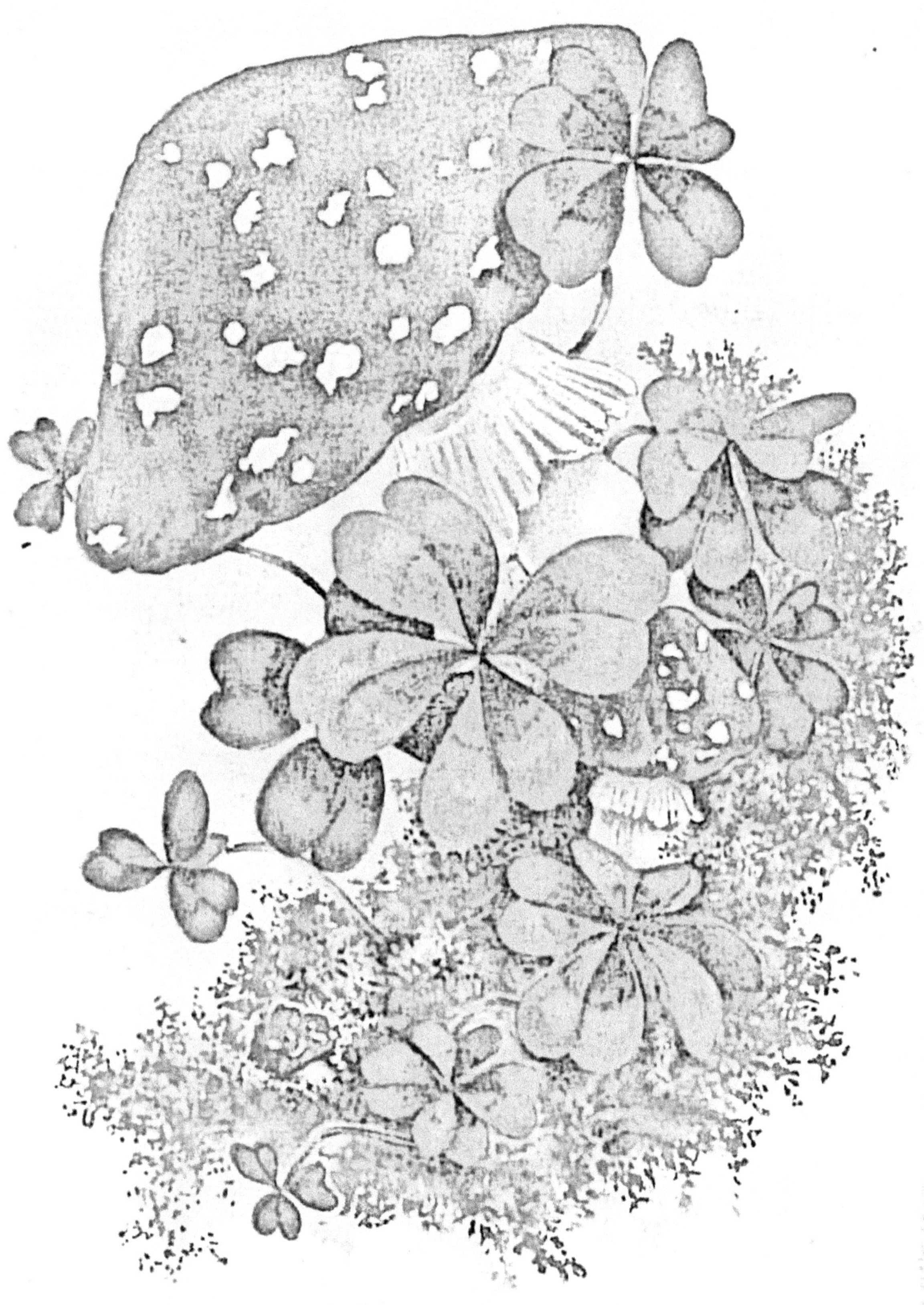

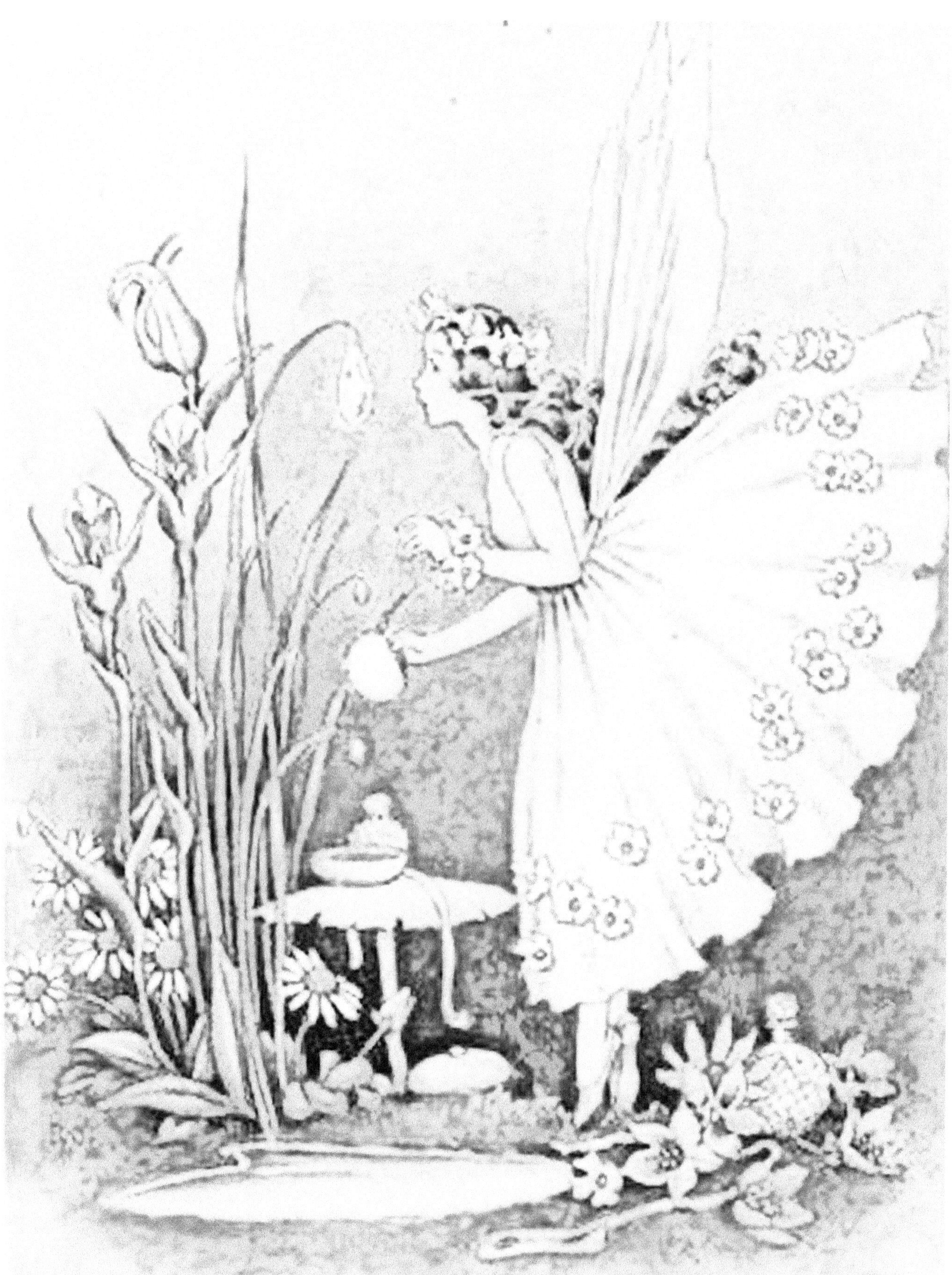

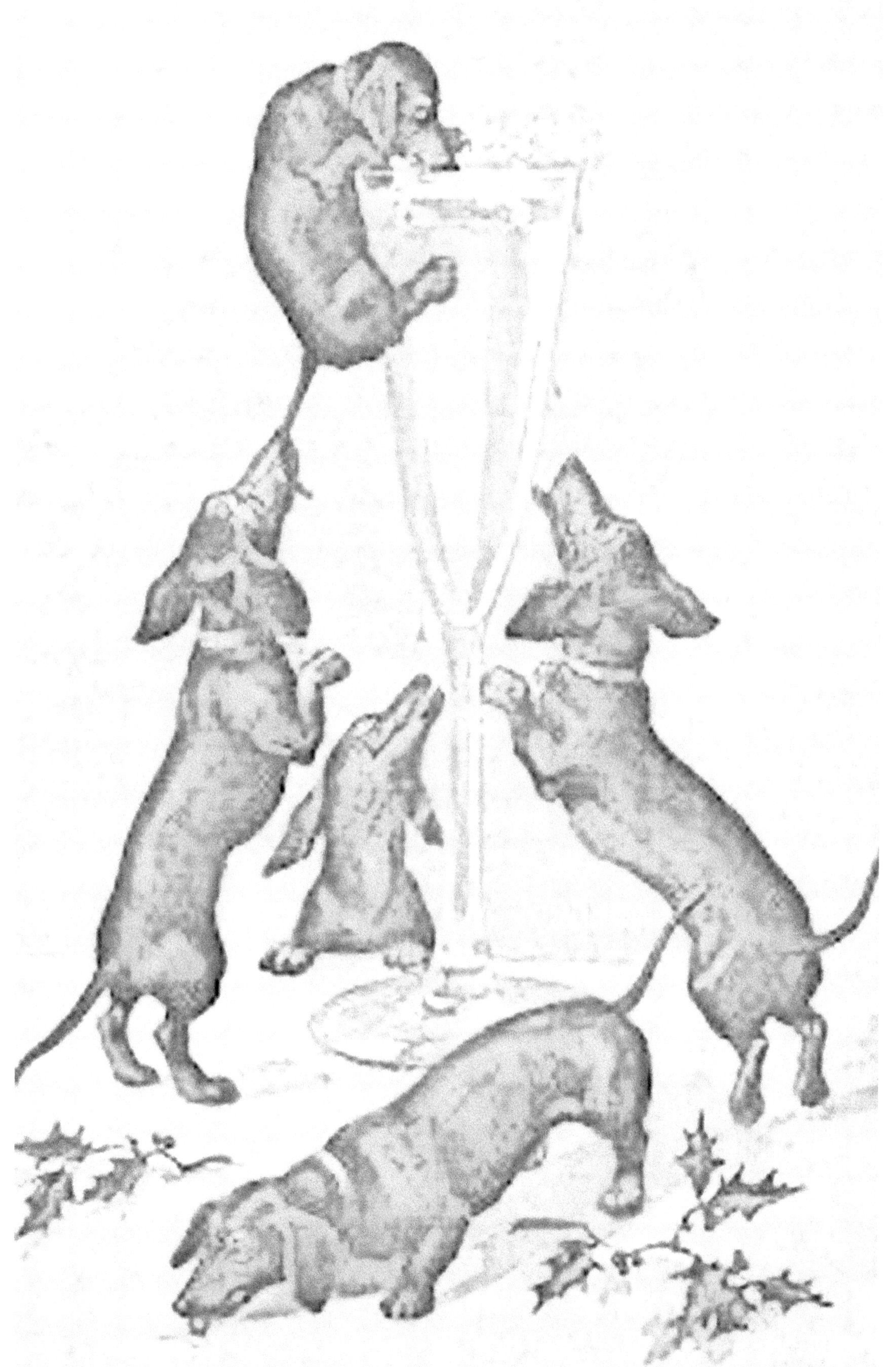

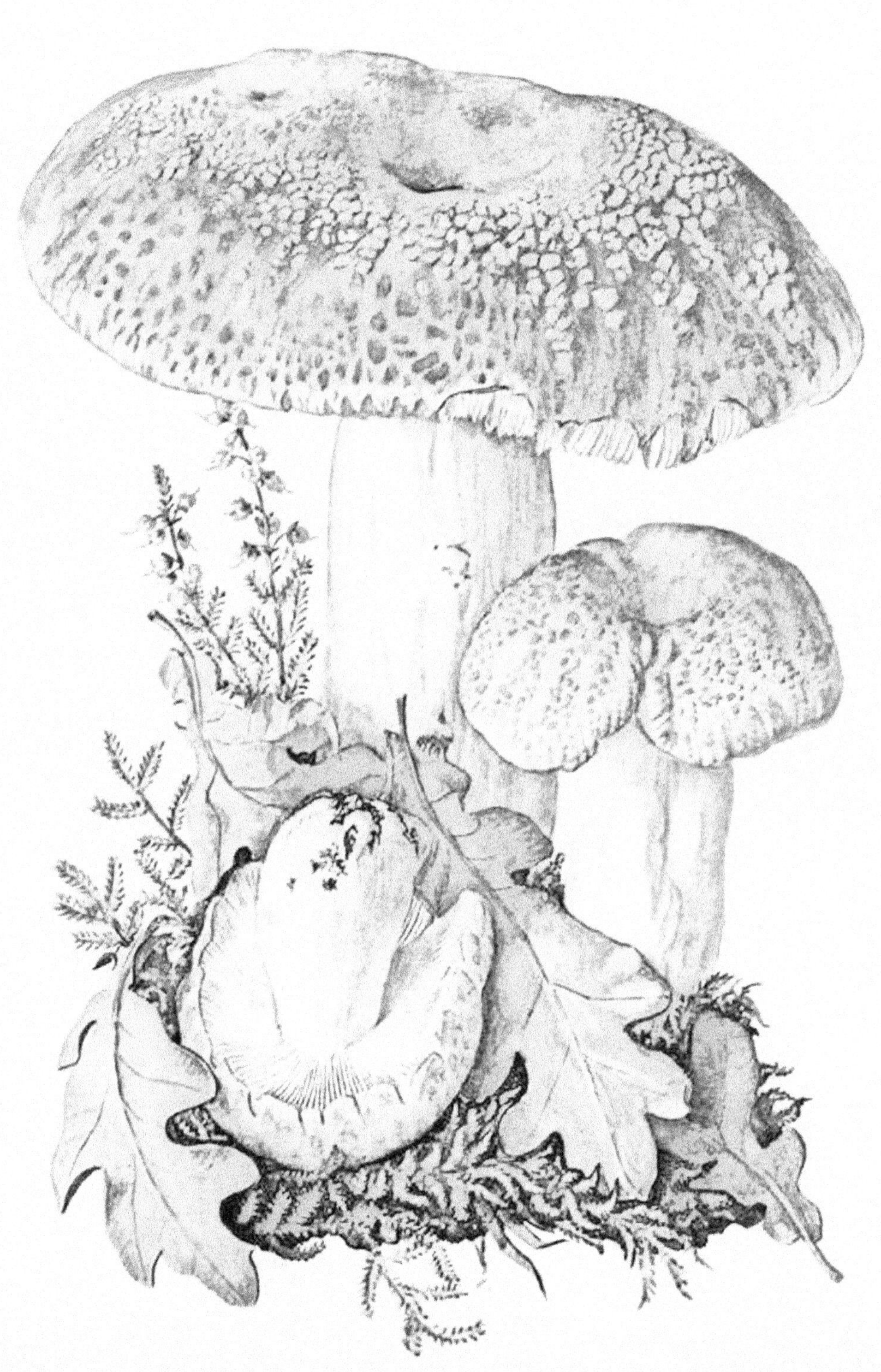

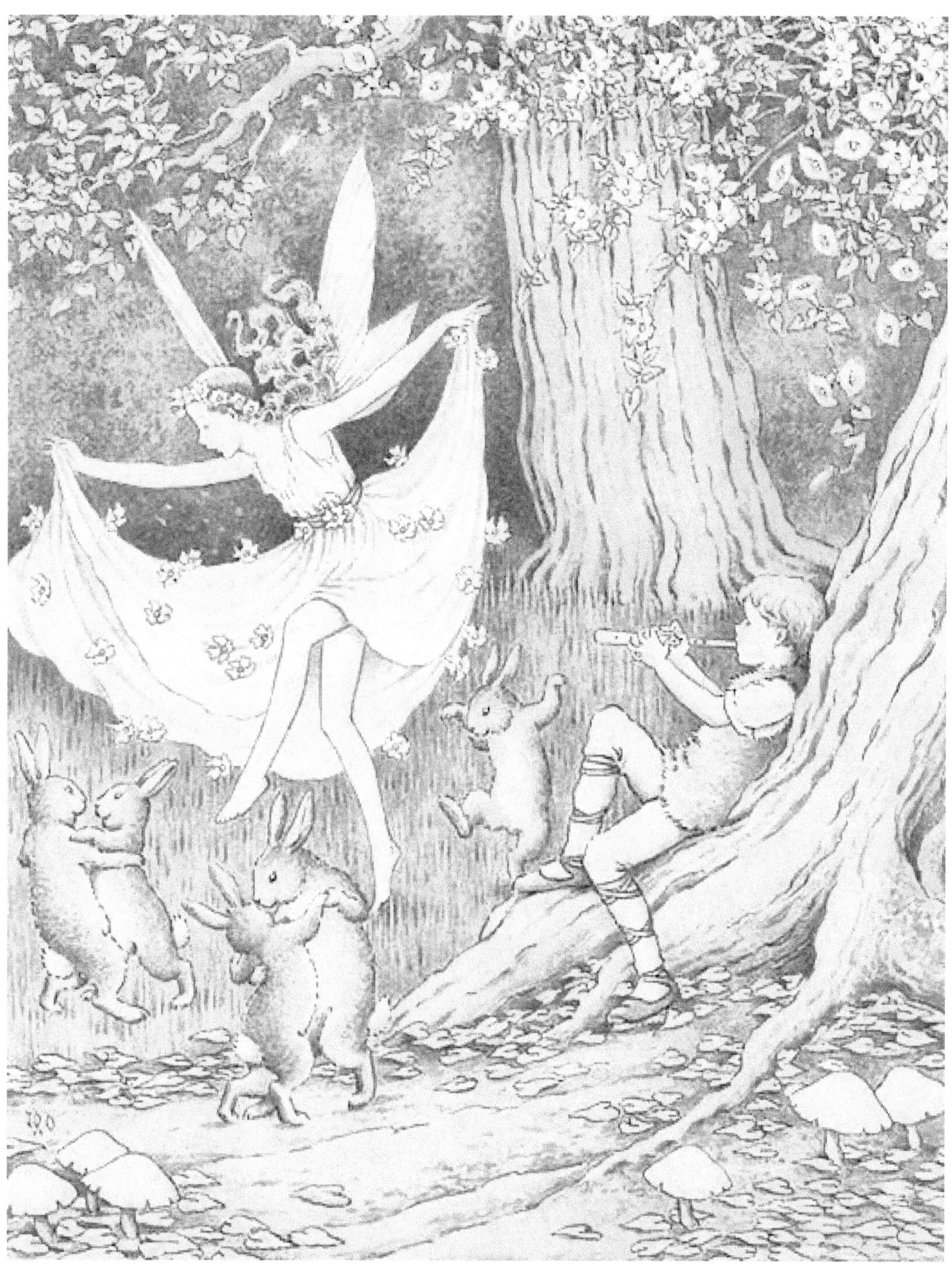

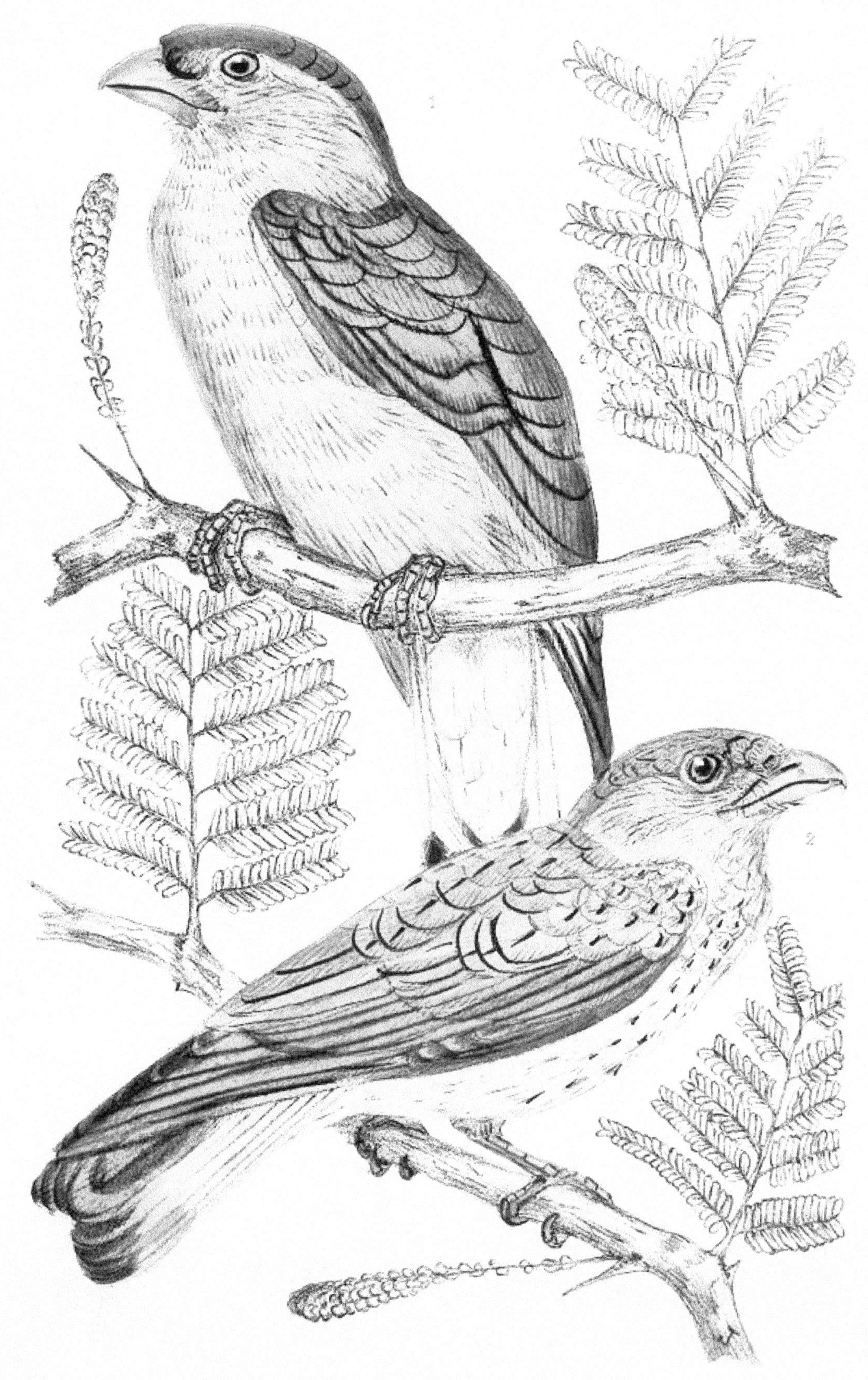

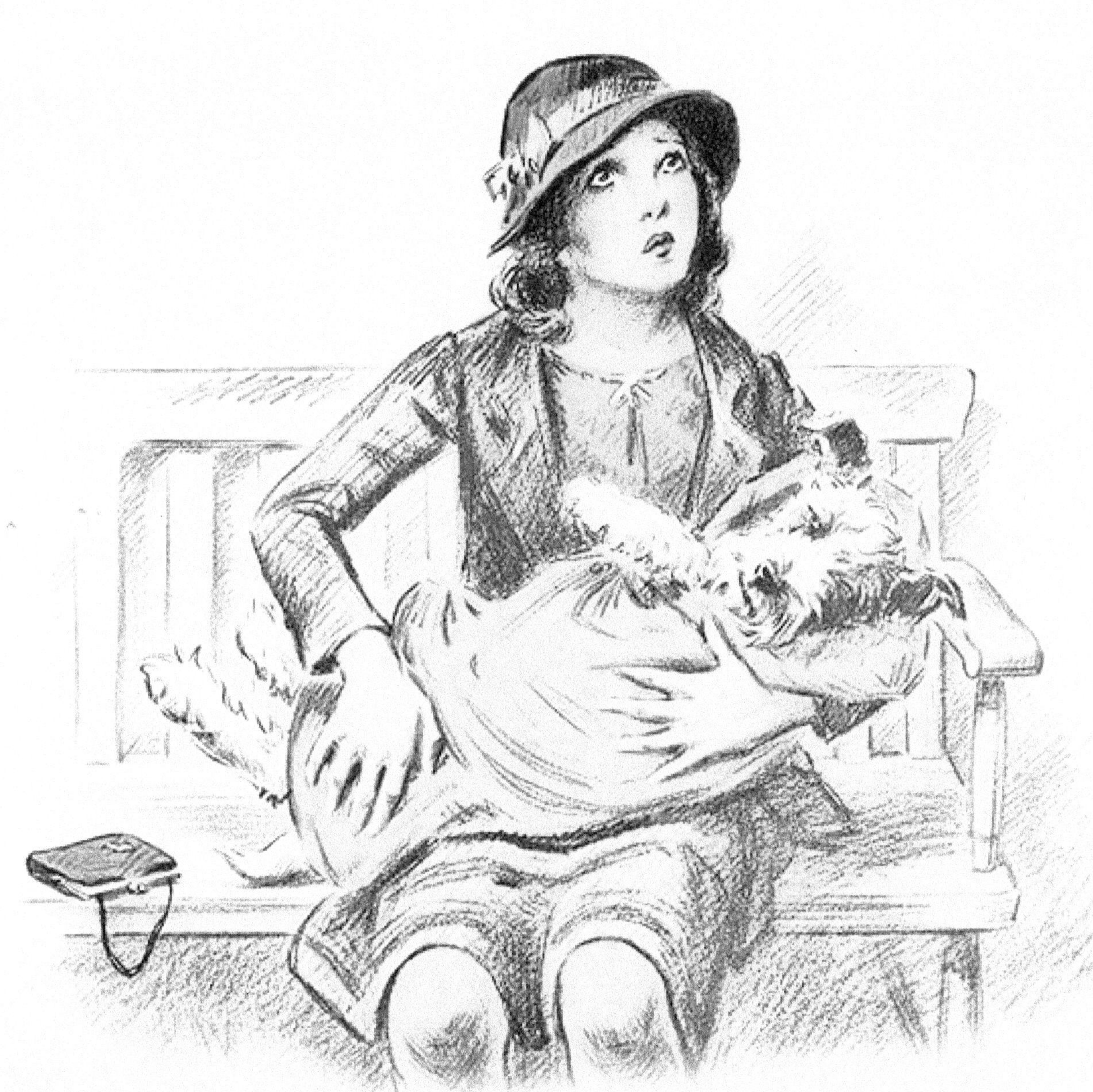

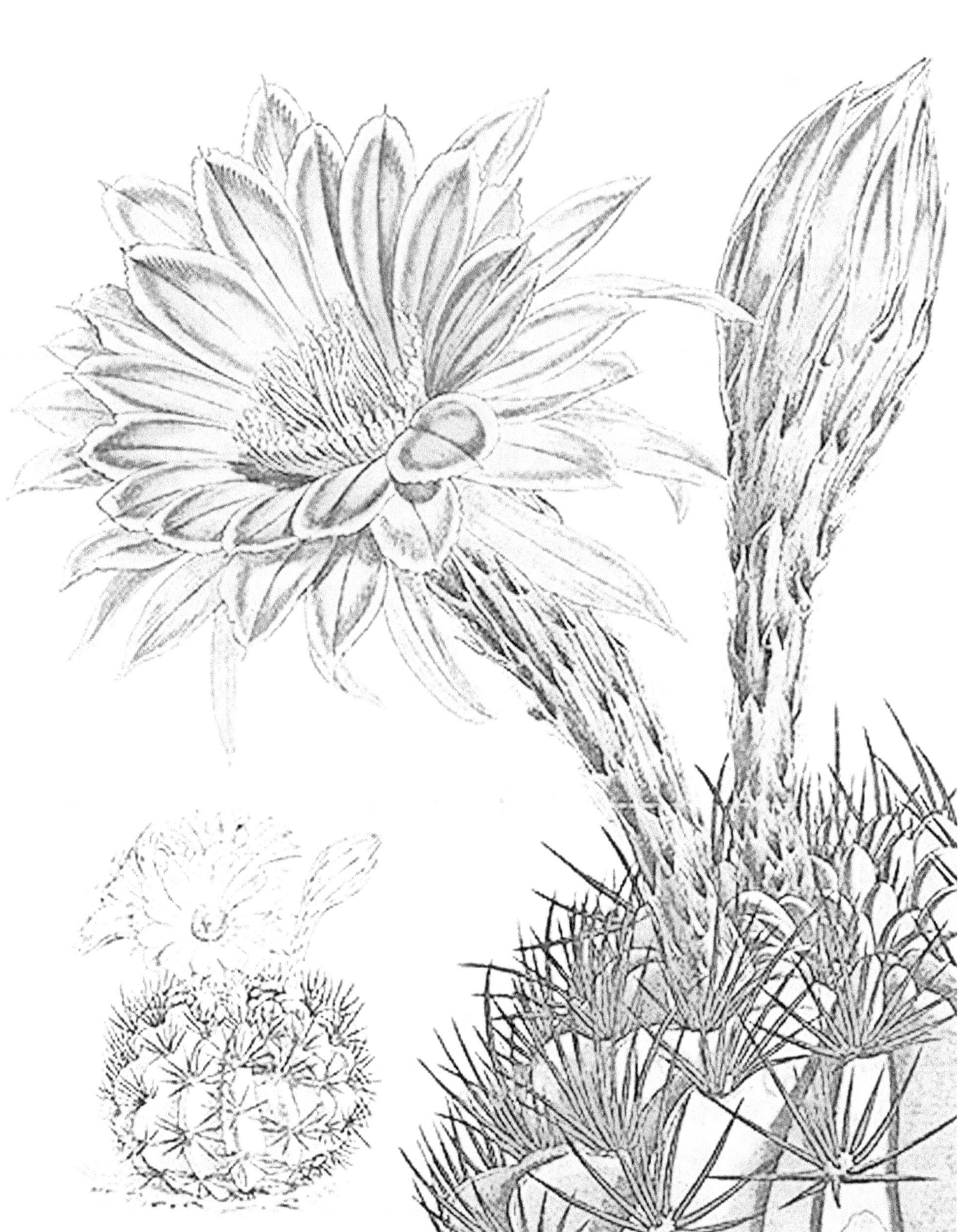

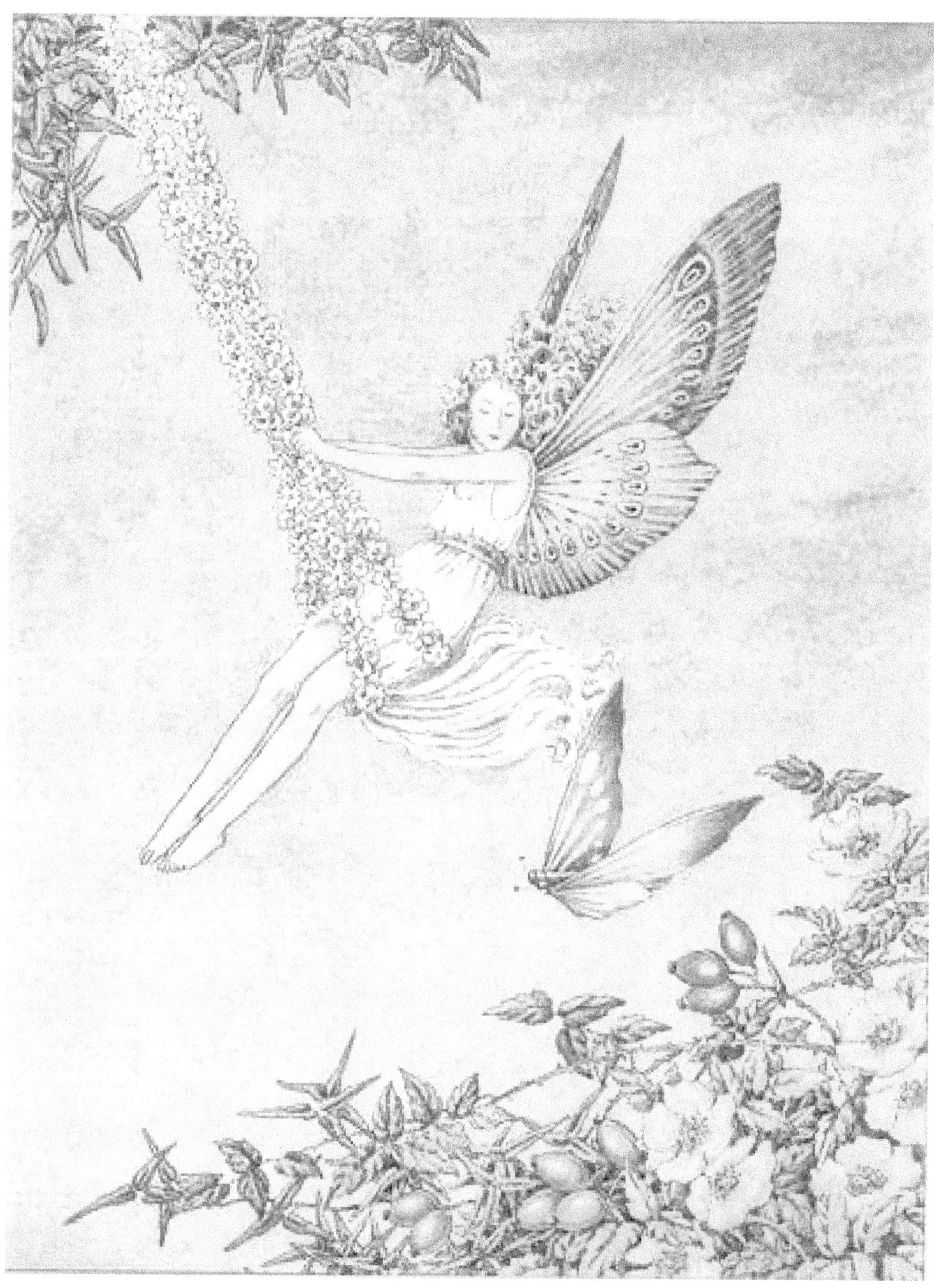

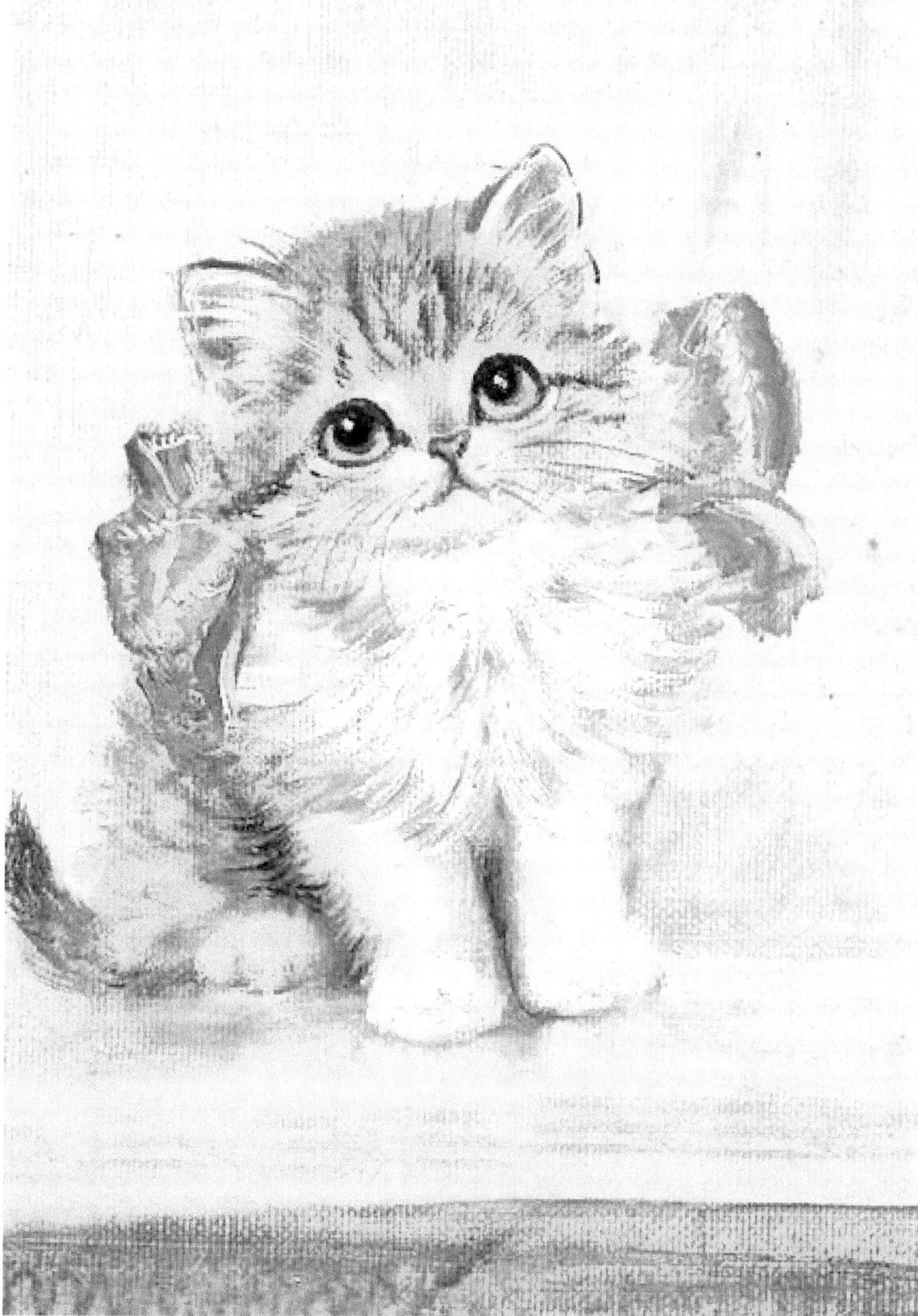

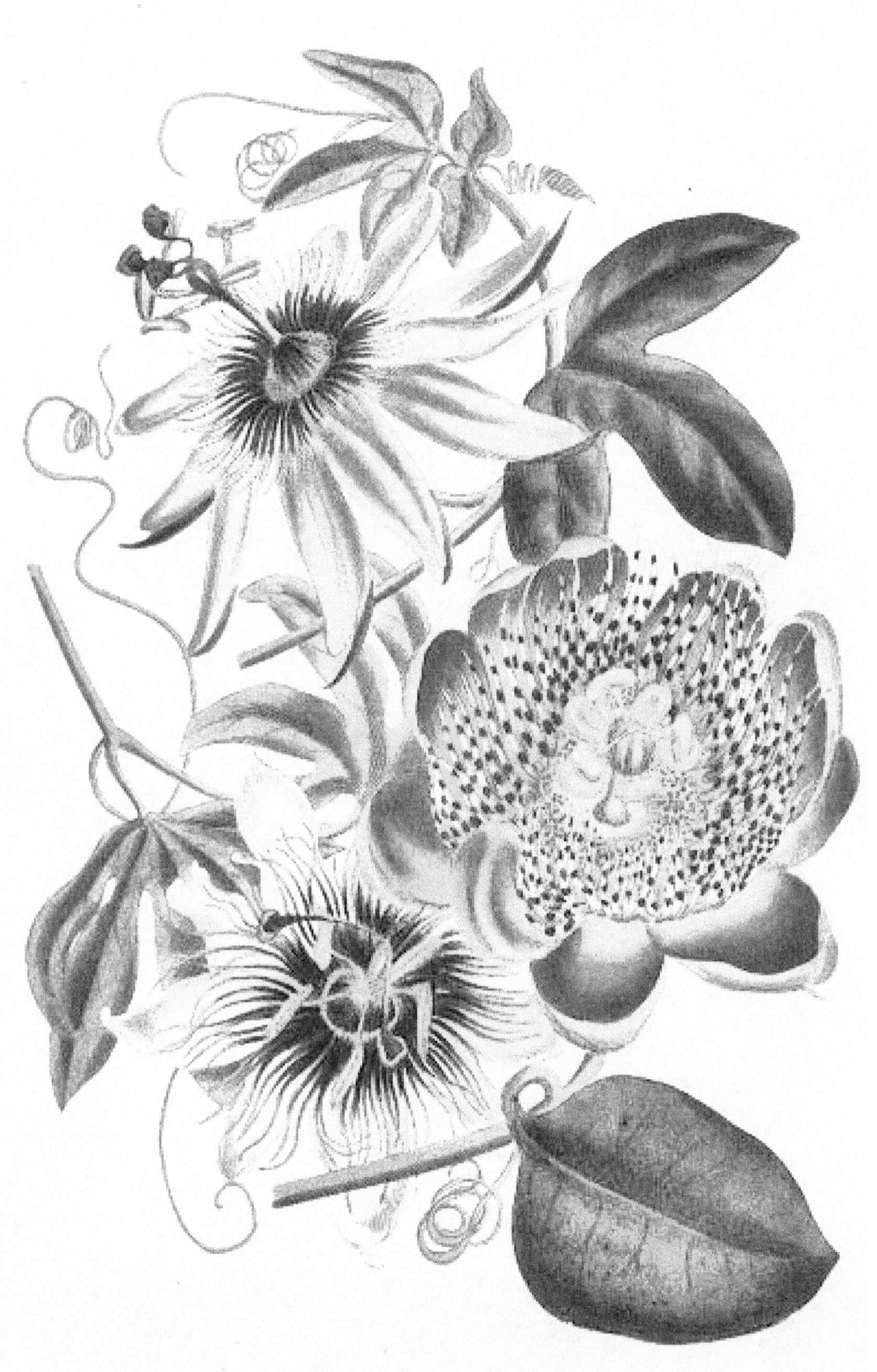

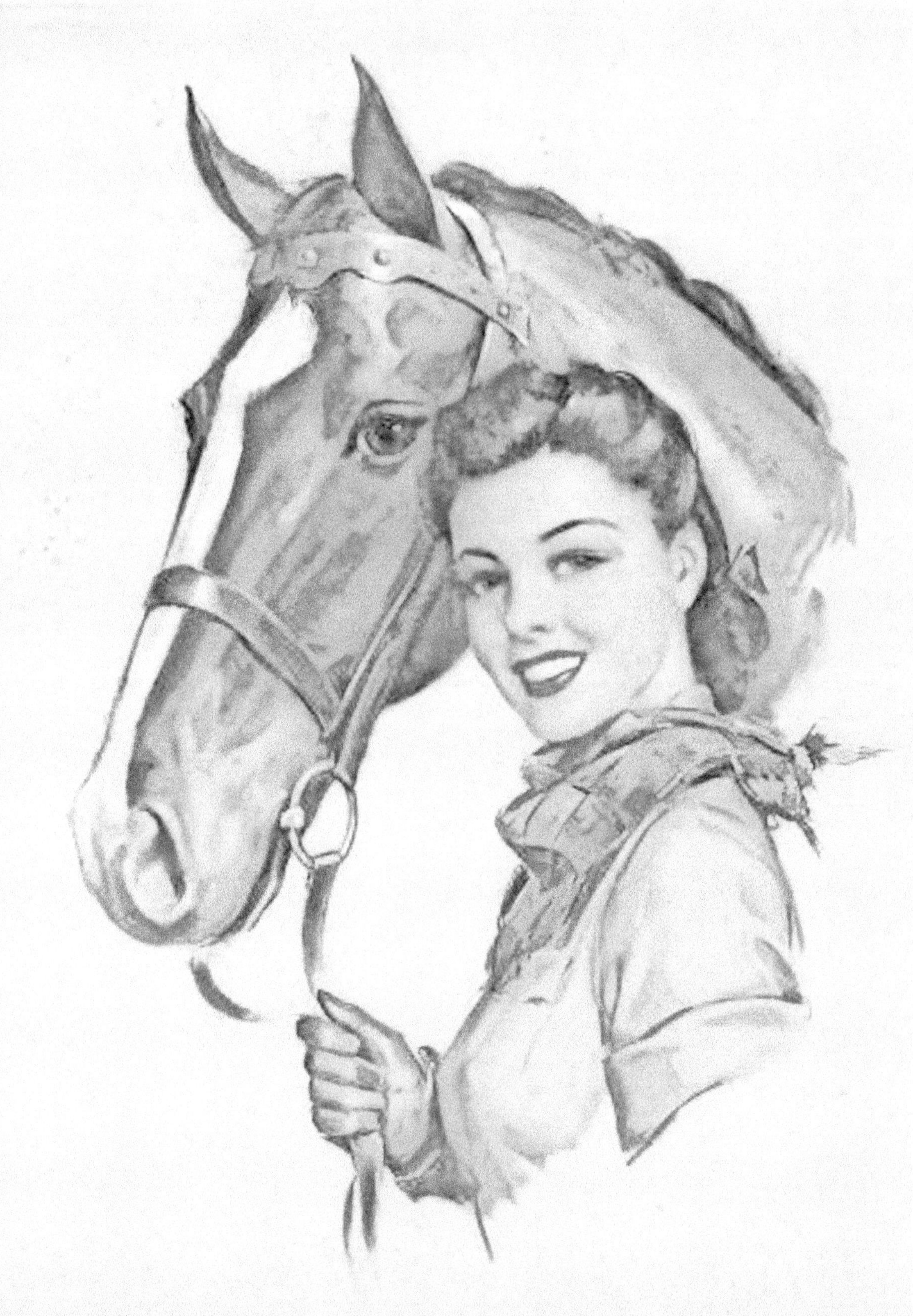

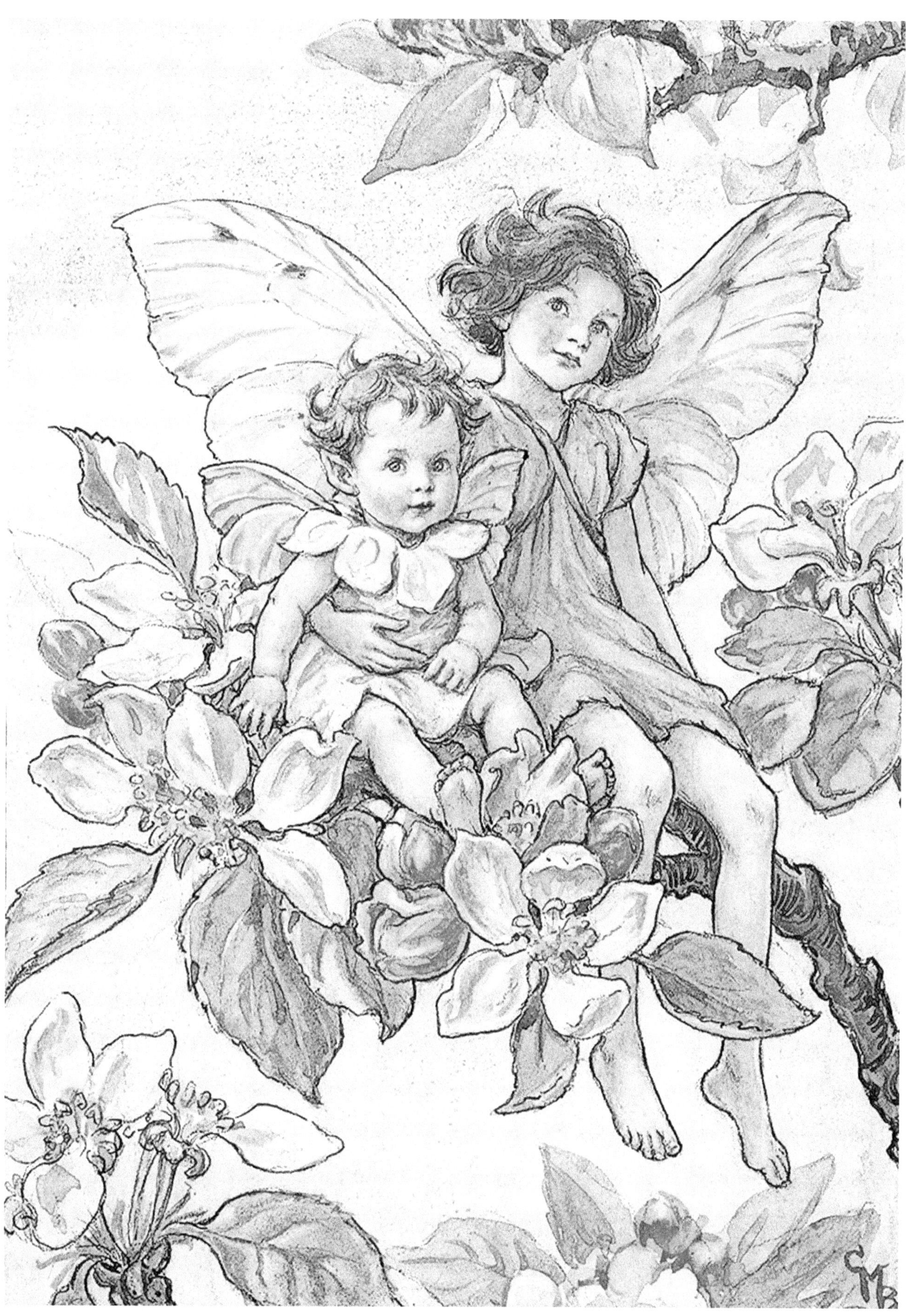

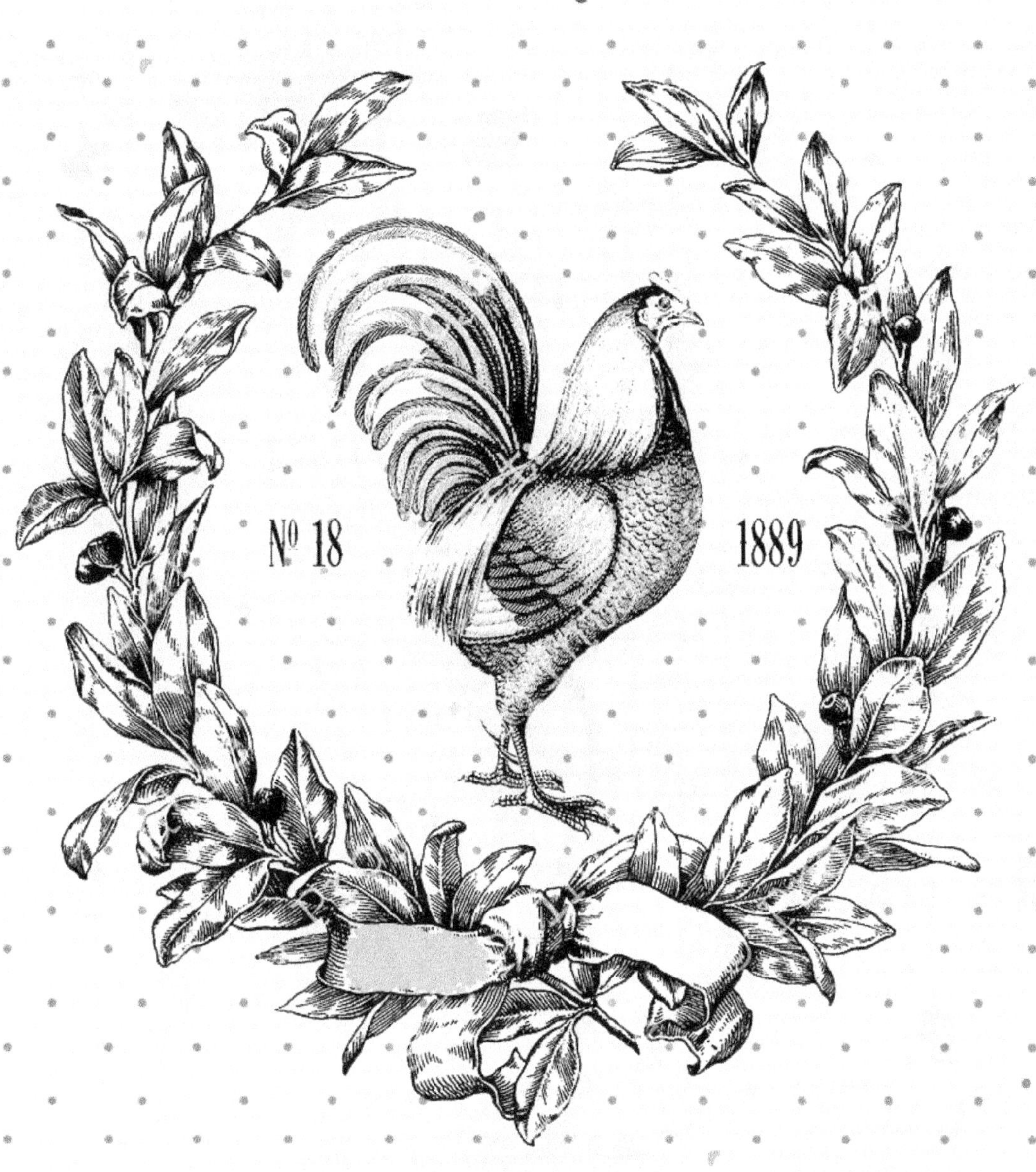

No 18
1889

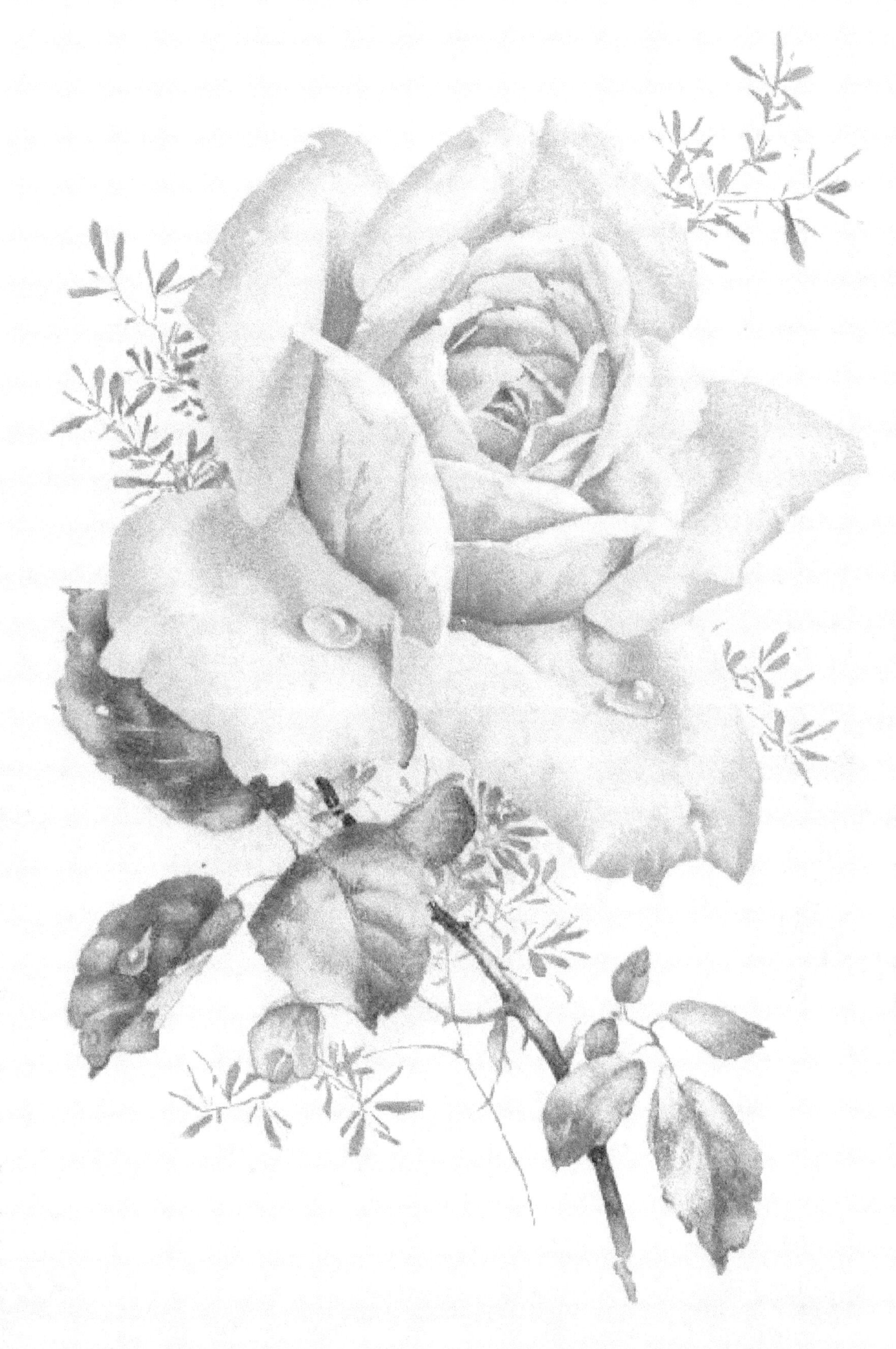

HAPPY Easter Day

Vintage

Easter Coloring book for adults

Grayscale Easter adult coloring books

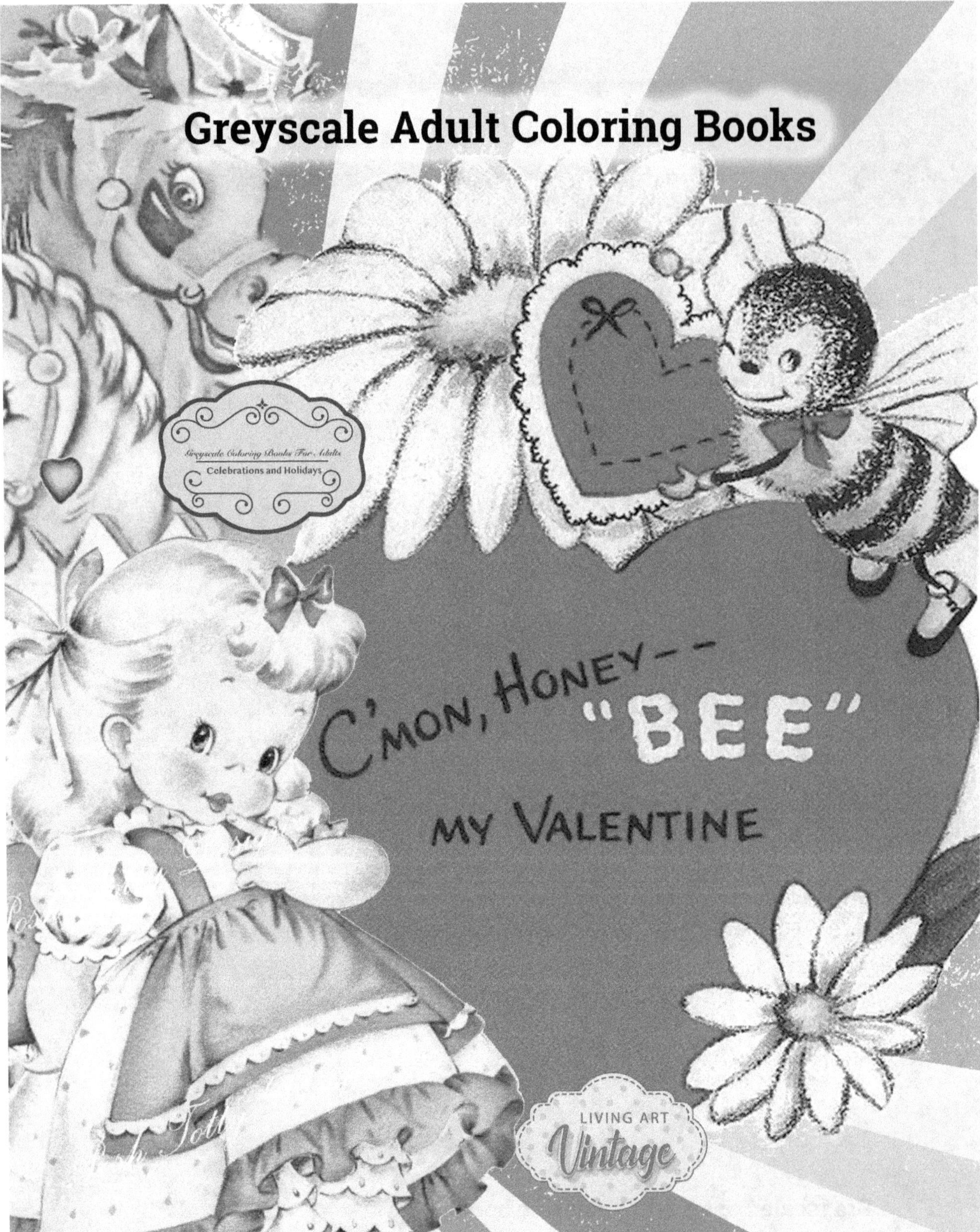

Greyscale Adult Coloring Books
Greyscale Coloring Books For Adults
Celebrations and Holidays
C'MON, HONEY-- "BEE" MY VALENTINE
LIVING ART
Vintage

Vintage

Boho

Coloring book

Greyscale coloring books for adults

Vintage
Butterfly
Coloring book

An Insect coloring book featuring authentic vintage images!

LIVING ART
Vintage

Butterflies coloring book for adults

www.ingramcontent.com/pod-product-compliance
Lightning Source LLC
LaVergne TN
LVHW080612200726

843509LV00007B/295